Concorde The Last Summer

Peter Marlow
Introduction by Mike Bannister
Foreword by A. A. Gill

Concorde **The Last Summer**

With 104 colour illustrations

Acknowledgments

This book is dedicated to my father, John Marlow, who taught me
from an early age to appreciate the beauty of engineering.

And to the many other people who made this work possible, in
particular Ian Cartlidge and Hector Pottie at Cartlidge Levene who
helped create the initial concept, Manchester Airport who let me
loose in G-BOAC, Peter Dyer for his helpful comments, Captain
Mark Hamwee who organized a trip to New York in Concorde for
my son Max and partner Fiona, which was the starting point for
the work, as I watched with my son Felix at the end of the runway
in amazement as G-BOAD flew over our heads on the way to
New York with a noise like thunder.

And all the many new friends I made near Heathrow during the
long summer of 2003 when I temporarily joined their community,
with a camera which was always pointed in the opposite direction
to theirs.

Any copy of this book issued by the publisher as a paperback is sold
subject to the condition that it shall not by way of trade or otherwise be
lent, resold, hired out or otherwise circulated without the publisher's
prior consent in any form of binding or cover other than that in which
it is published and without a similar condition including these words
being imposed on a subsequent purchaser.

First published in the United Kingdom in 2006 by
Thames & Hudson Ltd, 181A High Holborn, London WC1V 7QX

www.thamesandhudson.com

Concorde: The Last Summer © 2006 Thames & Hudson Ltd, London
Photographs © 2006 Peter Marlow/Magnum Photos www.petermarlow.com
The Last Flight © 2006 Mike Bannister

British Library Cataloguing-in-Publication Data
A catalogue record for this book is available from the British Library

ISBN-13: 978-0-500-51312-5
ISBN-10: 0-500-51312-0

Printed and bound in Hong Kong by Sing Cheong Printing Co. Ltd.

On the endpapers: details of Concorde aerial navigation charts
reproduced by kind permission of European Aeronautical Group UK Ltd

Foreword by **A. A. Gill**

I'm writing this at 30,000 feet, somewhere above a wine gum-coloured map where a little cartoon aeroplane skids across a flat earth with random names in English and Chinese floating below like clouds. I'm being carried from Sydney to London. The journey will take the best part of 24 hours. We will land – a nervous prediction, this – the day after the day we took off on. Somehow 12 hours in the air between Australia and England will have been given to us gratis: it is time that wouldn't exist on the ground, but up here it floats magically in the thin, blue, expandable air. My fellow passengers don't look terribly grateful to have been allotted a little extra bonus life, they look bored. They are watching movies and reading books, but mostly they are using sleep as an anaesthetic so that when they wake up the whole dull, uncomfortable interlude will be over. As far as I can tell, none of them is excitedly experiencing the astonishing physics of flight.

In a spare couple of generations, this thing – this machine – and its ability have become a humdrum bore, a necessary imposition. Even the gift of free extra time can't make it exciting. I have no idea what this plane is called, who built it, or where it comes from: it is one of the ugly, utilitarian family of gravid buses excused gravity. I have only ever recognized by sight, silhouette and voice two aeroplanes – the Spitfire and Concorde – and I only ever travelled in one.

When I flew Concorde, from Heathrow to New York, it stalled time. We landed to a second breakfast and the same cab driver, stuck in the same rush hour, driving on the other side of the road. But the anticipation and expectation were childlike, even for those who professed a world-weary air of boredom. Concorde defied familiarity. You got to the airport with smiley sprightliness, all grins and chat at the special check-in, with its petits snobberies of the Concorde-branded boarding cards and luggage labels: no airline bothers to print 'Jumbo' or 'Airbus' on their tickets. There was the camaraderie at the lounge, the cocktail chat with the captain, and then there was the flight: the momentary surprise at the smallness of the cabin, the narrowness of the leg-room and then, strangely, a predictable sameness. Up front the display told us when we reached Mach 2, and we knew that outside the sound barrier was being sundered in rolling thunder across the Earth, but inside the display might as well have said 'toilet occupied'. Flying Concorde was the same as flying anything else but noisier and quicker. What I do remember, though, was the view from the tiny window of the curvature of the earth with the dark sky above: Concorde cleaved the icing of the atmosphere.

I once interviewed Tony Benn, who as the British Minister for Technology in the 1960s had championed Concorde, when he retired from the House of Commons. He said his abiding achievements as a minister were the rationalization of maps, nuclear power stations and Concorde. What, I asked, had made him continue with this ludicrously expensive project, which would only be afforded by subsidized capitalists and the undeserving rich? 'Well,' he said, 'I thought why should the military be the only people to go supersonic?' Why, indeed? Concorde's thin fuselage was crammed with national romance and hubris.

I only flew in Concorde once, but actually I travelled with it hundreds of times in west London. We would hear it in the early evening and look up at the elegant, fabulous, dart-like silhouette. It never ceased to please, like seeing a particularly good example of Romanesque architecture or a Georgian teapot floating by.

In this book Peter Marlow has captured the last summer of Concorde seen through the eyes of the people who really flew in her. It was those on the ground who looked up and felt that moment of weightless awe, and, for a fleeting moment, were once again like a child in bed staring up at Airfix models hanging from the ceiling. They were the real passengers of Concorde. It was only from the outside that you got the true heart-skipping brilliance of this supersonic dart. The journey it made was in our heads.

Spotters of all sorts court smirks and easy ridicule from those of us who don't look and don't 'hobby'. What is so particularly and characteristically touching about this collection of images is that Peter never for a moment views the Concorde-spotters with anything other than human respect. There are no sneering invitations to snigger, no smart, brittle irony. Peter makes us complicit spotter-spotters. In these quiet and elegiac pictures are feelings that can be simultaneously both profound and prosaic, and that is Peter's great gift as a photographer – to see the world in a grain of sand, with astute peripheral vision, a spotter of the moment between moments.

Peter and I have worked together a number of times. Once, in a crude, forgotten Soviet industrial and military midden on the Baltic coast, Peter insisted on using an old-fashioned Rolleiflex camera, which he perched on his tummy and looked down into. It was very slow. Why didn't he have an SLR camera, I huffed. Because, he explained quietly, the people he was photographing 'were nervous of having their photographs taken'. They associated it with the secret police: pointing lenses and motor drives at them was intrusive and rude. Peter has always had a telling respect for his subjects: it is the original and finest quality of photojournalism, a quality which shows in his images of the static – but somehow eccentrically Homeric – journeys of these witnesses to Concorde's last summer, a record of so many armchair Icaruses.

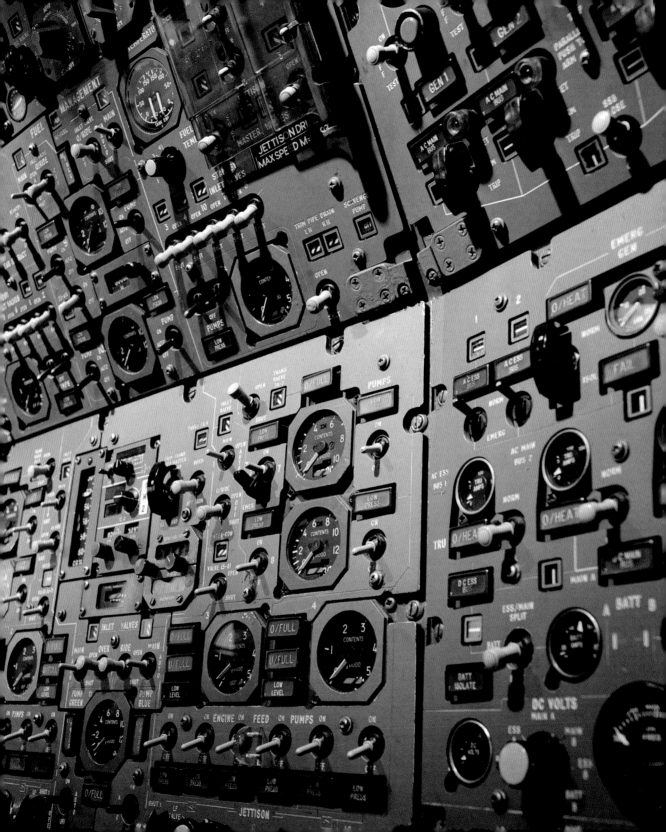

The Last Flight **Mike Bannister**

April 9th 1969. I was in the study room at the College of Air Training in Hamble, England, swotting for my final exams, when, on a little black and white television in the corner, I saw Concorde fly for the first time. It was the first flight of the British-built prototype 002: Brian Trubshaw was waving, Raymond Baxter was talking, and it seemed the whole country was watching. I'd always wanted to be a pilot – right from the age of seven when I used to sit on the beach at Bournemouth on the south coast of England and watch small aircraft flying to France. I hate coach journeys and it had taken 5½ long hours to get there from Luton. I thought that if I was in one of those aircraft I could have done it in 20 minutes. In that college study room, my mind was set again, I knew what I wanted to do: I wanted to be a Concorde pilot.

By 1977, the year after Concorde entered public service, my chance had arrived. I was fortunate enough to have two stints flying Concorde: from 1977 to 1989 as a co-pilot and latterly as an instructor, and from 1995 to 2003 as Chief Concorde Pilot. When the call came in 1995, I was stunned and delighted. I'd been so lucky to have 13 years flying this fabulous aircraft and she'd given me memories to hold to the end of my career. I thought I'd 'had my go' and now it was someone else's turn. I said I would have to think about the offer, which I did...for about a millisecond!

Friday, 24 October 2003

> *'Speedbird Two – contact Heathrow Director now, frequency 134.97, and welcome home for the last time.'*

Operating a supersonic aircraft with 100 passengers and 11 crew across the Atlantic safely, efficiently, smoothly and to a precise schedule tends to focus the mind! It wasn't really until 24 October 2003, when the British Air Traffic Controller (ATC) said '... welcome home for the last time', that I began to truly comprehend what we were about to do – retire a perfectly serviceable beauty of an aircraft. On that trip we had done so much. We had been to the edge of space, where the sky above turned darker and you could see the curvature of the Earth. We had travelled at Mach 2 – a ground speed of over 1,390 mph, 23 miles a minute, a mile every

2.6 seconds. We had flown faster than a rifle bullet; faster than the Earth rotates. We literally 'bought back time', doing in two days what would otherwise have taken four.

But now all of that was coming to an end and, while I fully understood the irrefutable commercial logic and the need to take some very difficult decisions in a post 9/11 airline business and world, this was beginning to feel emotional.

As Rod Eddington, the Chief Executive of British Airways had said:

'...It was a difficult decision, and a very sad one, certainly one of the most difficult I have had to make during my time with the airline. Sadly, even the greatest of stories have to have a final chapter. That final chapter has come sooner than we would have hoped.'

The last flight from JFK to Heathrow seemed rather surreal. A pre-flight news conference broadcast across the world, photographs, handshakes, smiles and tears. There was even a multicoloured water arch and flag-waving as Concorde G-BOAG (Alpha Golf) taxied towards the runway. Not to mention the precise timing! We had to start our take-off roll at 11h 37m 50s BST exactly to ensure that, on arrival at Heathrow, we could join up with two other Concordes. Our 'stream of three' landing needed to be perfectly synchronized. The overwhelming feeling was that this was something special. There had been so many good wishes during the day, from the public, the media, the 100 celebrities, business people and prize-winners on board, as well as from ATC and other aircraft crew, to name a few. As our afterburners roared us down Runway 31L at JFK, one US pilot called us on the radio: 'Go, Concorde, go. We'll sure miss you.' It was the last time this wonderful aircraft would do what she was built to do. This was the end.

'Alpha Golf' carried us across the Atlantic in her usual uneventful way, unaware that this was her last scheduled flight. As we were vectored overhead Heathrow Airport, the ATC Centre at West Drayton, then northern and eastern London, there were more and more messages of goodwill over the radio. Before I really knew it we were turned on to a heading of 250 degrees to intercept the final approach path to Runway 27R. We went down to 2,500 feet for the final run-in over the centre of the city before we started to descend on the glideslope.

The authorities had, understandably, urged the public to stay away from Heathrow for fear of 'Concorde-spotters' bringing the airport to a congested halt. Although there were many thousands there, Concorde's greatest fans, the public, had generally listened – and how. Instead of travelling west to the airport it seemed as if millions had lined the roads under our flight path: it was like flying down the Mall with the Red Arrows for the Queen's Golden Jubilee all over again. Vehicles pulled over, people waved, and the flags and fireworks were all so impressive and moving. But what touched me most of all was seeing 'White Van Man's' unexpected tribute. I remember it so vividly to this day. He'd pulled his all-pervading tormentor of the family motorist to the side of the road, blocking the way for any who might have dared to try to move at this historic moment. Then he'd climbed on to his roof and was now frantically waving one of the largest Union Flags I've ever seen. He seemed to speak for everyone.

Closer to Heathrow now and I could see our two sister Concordes ahead of us. Our 'stream of three' landing was to be broadcast live, which kind of concentrates the mind on the touchdown once more! I called 'Gear down – landing checks' to lower the undercarriage for landing, and then it dawned on me: this was the final time. After 27 years of supersonic service this was the last time that Concorde would ever land at her home base. Those wheels would never be moved again in commercial service.

Through 300 feet, fully stabilized and a mile to go, down to 100 feet and I could begin to hear the distinctive and unique rush of air as Concorde entered 'ground effect'. The Flight Engineer calls: 50, 40, 30, 20, 15. The autothrottles are out, I reduce power smoothly, pull back on the control column to hold the attitude, check, check, check, kick off the drift from the northerly wind and we were down. 1606 BST, spot on time – the last ever commercial landing of the world's greatest airliner. I was proud but so sad at the same time.

We formed up with our sister Concordes, 'Alpha Echo', which had flown from Edinburgh, and 'Alpha Fox', which had flown a circular route from Heathrow, for a photocall from the air and on the ground, with flags flying out of the movable flight-deck windows. Then there was a 'lap of honour' around Heathrow before disembarking and facing the world's media on a huge temporary stand where we joined two other Concordes to create a parked formation of five.

En route the Heathrow Fire Service had also planned a multi-appliance, valedictory water arch for us to taxi under. The drill was easy: approach the arch with the flag out of the flight-deck window, within 100 yards of the arch bring the flag in, close and lock the window, taxi Concorde under the arch, open the window, put the flag out. Few know what actually happened to me: flag in, close window, window jammed, under water arch, thousands of gallons of water through window, pilot drenched. Having parked Concorde, there was a distinctive squelching sound from my shoes as I walked up for the first interview with Richard Quest of CNN.

More interviews followed, along with a chance to chat to people and a reception for the 'Concorde Family' – all those at British Airways who had done so much to keep this wonderful aircraft safely in the air during 27 years of supersonic operations. The Chairman of British Airways, Lord Marshall, spoke eloquently as ever and captured many of our feelings:

> *'Concorde is a wonderful aircraft and her last day is one of mixed emotions. Everyone has enormous pride in all that she has achieved but there is inevitable sadness that we have to move on and say farewell.'*

Then, for me, a highlight: a photograph of the Concorde Family in front of our fleet of aircraft. Both they and we gathered together for the very last time.

Then back to the reception for fond farewells, hand presses, hugs and kisses. My bags had been taken from me just after we parked and were already in my car. So, at the end of the formalities, when I was left pretty much alone, I just opened the small door in the side of the hangar and strolled across the tarmac to drive home. It was getting really cold and quite misty and the floodlights had a sodium-yellow tinge to them. Now completely alone, I walked across slowly, then stopped. There was just me and five of the most beautiful machines man has ever built.

The Last Summer was over.

Dana Church (46) Animator

'It's poetry of technology....'

David Lewis (16) Schoolboy, from Somerset

'I flew to New York in it.... It's a shame the journey doesn't take longer....'

Nick Green and Scott Lewis (17) Engineer and RAF photographer

'Sorry to see history passing by....'

Graham Hill (39) Computer consultant

*'It's just on my way back from work. It's a shame it's being retired,
and a shame [Richard] Branson won't take it over.'*

[Name withheld]

[Name withheld] Hotel worker at Heathrow Airport, from Denmark

Graham Alexander (50) Sales director of a security company

'I flew Concorde four times. I'm sad to see it go and I wanted to be part of that history of it going.'

Brian Bicknell (58) British Airways worker (retired)

'They should keep it going. There are still plenty of millionaires left....
I'm disgusted they won't sell it to the highest bidder.'

Minoru Ishibashi (38) Airport worker at Narita Airport, Tokyo

'I came to see Concorde for memory shots....'

Steve Patman (47) Electrician

'I've been spotting for thirty-five years. She'll be sadly missed. Every time I see her I still get a buzz.'

Mrs L. Brown (53) Civil servant

'I always wanted to go on it. Now I'll never have the chance.'

Mrs E. Thomas (78) Worker on Concorde wiring looms (retired)

'I went on it as a Christmas treat from my grandson in 2001.
I feel sorry that it's going because it was a wonderful experience...it really was.'

Martin Taylor (36) Software manager

*'I flew on it three weeks ago as a lifetime ambition.
I normally come here with my three-year-old triplets.
How do I explain to them that it's no longer flying?'*

Ahmed Majothi British Airways car-park attendant at Heathrow Airport

*'It's one of the very beautiful planes....
It makes all our alarms go off when it takes off.'*

Max Naylor Marlow (9) Schoolboy

'I went on it in April.... It was great... but I didn't like the lobster....'

Arthur Backshall Passenger Assistant for Lufthansa at Heathrow Airport

'The taxpayers built it and paid for it. I'm sad to see it go. It turns heads wherever it goes....
You can't move here on weekends for people, all after Concorde.'

Mary Field (40) Clerical worker

'I blame the French....'

Nick Field (46) IT manager

'I am not a plane-spotter, I am a Concorde-spotter.'

Colin McCarthy (40) Storeman

'Just a great shame that it's passing. I wanted to see it just one last time.'

Rob King (54) Deputy headmaster

*'I was on a training course in Basingstoke about behaviour in schools
and couldn't resist coming. Once it's gone, it's gone –
it's the last time Joe Public will go supersonic.'*

Richard Heaney (56) British Airways ramp worker

'Our son was born 21 January 1976, the day it first took passengers.'

Stuart Mackintosh (40) Accountant

'I've had a stressful week. I used to do this fifteen years ago...
coming here takes my mind off things and it's on the way back from work.
I'm disappointed to see it go... shame they haven't developed it further.
By the time my little one grows up, she won't be able to hear the
noise of it taking off.'

Sarah Saunders Customer service manager

'It's criminal to take it out of the sky.'

Mathew Lowe (37) Care assistant

'I've come down for five days from Manchester.'

Alan Gunner (45) Fire detection engineer

'Better to retire it gracefully than suddenly pack up.'

Bridget Gunner (52) Housewife

'It's just an amazing plane.... It makes your heart shake.'

Alex Bayou (15) Schoolboy

'Richard Branson should buy 'em....'

Brian Lafbery (56) Health service worker (retired)

'This is not my main hobby.... I do trains.'

Lukas Lusser (37), from Basel Law School

*'If you see it, it was born to fly. If any aircraft ever
looked like it belonged in the sky, then it is Concorde.'*

Milo Kalerer (41) Printer, from Switzerland

'... pity it never came to Zurich.'

Chris Coles (60) Taxi driver

*'I saw it before it entered service at the Paris Air Show in the sixties
and have been following it ever since.'*

Peter Leigh (56) Security at News International

'I was on a test flight with Brian Trubshaw and we did some aerobatics in Concorde with a Phantom fighter. The Phantom couldn't keep up.... Branson should get hold of it.'

Chris Ball (35) Auditor

*'It's a piece of history, consigned to the past...
like the Routemaster bus.'*

Tim Stephens (58) Retired biologist

'I am not a plane-spotter... I just love Concorde.'

Peter Johnson (21) Chauffeur and student with father **Nick** (57)

*'A masterpiece of engineering, unforgettable. My dad gave me a
1:100 model as a memento for my 21st birthday.'*

Trevor Wright Taxi driver for 'The Wright Brothers'

'I've seen every Concorde ever built and photographed them all.'

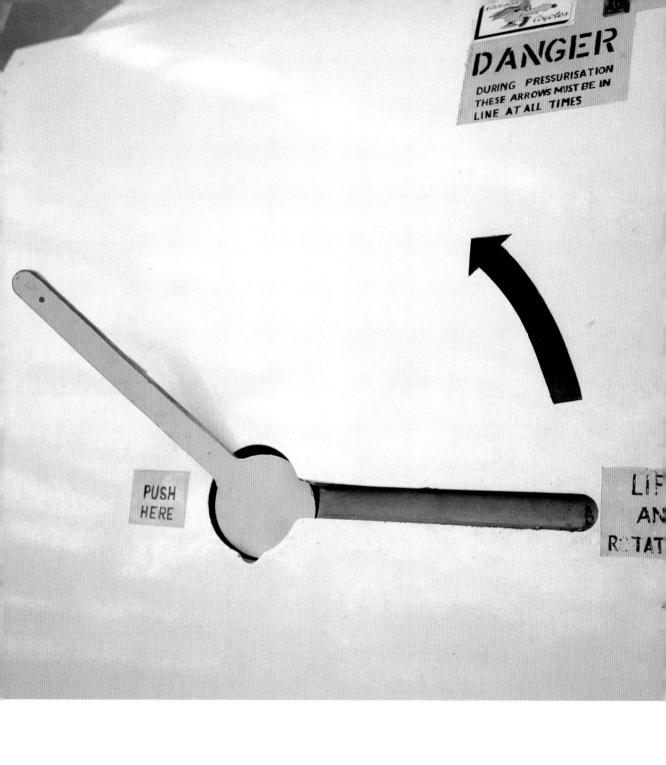

Steve Kurtz (50) Banker, from Florida, USA

'I came in August and didn't get a good picture, so I went to JFK last week, but the weather was bad. I then went to Washington DC for the farewell flight, but it was an utterly awful day, so I'm back here again. It's now or never as it's not going to fly anymore.'

Mark and Patricia Canning with children **Lawrence and Christian**

'I like the sound and the pointy nose....' **(Christian)**

Julia Zuk (50) Bank worker

'It's the most beautiful thing flying. If this was America they wouldn't let this happen.... I will be in tears when it lands... I left my mascara off today.'

MA-02803	125	
OE-GEO	125	⌣
C-FIMD	125	
N440TC	G-IV	⌣
NIBAN ①	G-IV	
N900LS	G-IV	
N66ALC	CL-60	
N900Q	DC-9 EX	⌣
N105Y	CK-III	
N7 ①	G-V	
EC-HLD	✓ CVF, SWT (DH-C13) ⌣	

LHR ⌒

VGOA	346, VS ('Indian Princess') ⌣
9V-SFJ	74F, SQ ⌣
HB-IKR	G-IV (Be.+ Ed-ciP) (1630-1909)
HL7423	74F, OZ
VMEC' (+05)	346, VS ⌣
MEDH	* 320, (UF-c13) ⌣

JY-JAV	3.12, ZW-AIR (W-c13) ⌣
I-FJIN	Do.50 (−1759) ⌣
N663UA	763, UA
OH-LZE	* 321, AY ⌣
EC-ILO	321, IB ⌣
JA-205J	77.2, JL (new c13) ⌣
EC-HRQ	125 (139-
CS-TNM	320, TP
V 'GE'	346, VS ⌣
C- ✦ 1657	703, AC
	✦ 320, HELLAS JET 305
VH-OEC	744, QF ⌣
B-HXN	343, CX ⌣
SB-	✦332, CY ('nnno____')

OS-09 f. ⌒

LHR ⌒

VF 'OX'	346, VS	⌣

Craig Tiley (20) Student

'Irreplaceable.'

[Name withheld]

Neil Evans (56) Estimator

'My father worked on the Comet and I've been watching aircraft since I was a nipper.
This one has something extra. Apart from the Spitfire it's the most perfect-shaped
aircraft that has ever flown. It's another one of our icons that's disappeared
under the reign of Tony Blair.'

Mary Heaney (53) Slough housewife

*'I'm a Barry Manilow fan and you know what they say about
his nose and Concorde...but I love them both.'*

Sue Rimmer (57) Beach-bum (retired)

'I met John [Harris] four years ago and we both love planes....
As a child, instead of having dolls I had a set of Spitfires.'

John Harris (63) Electronic engineer (formerly worked on Concorde)

*'I worked on the testing of the prototype at Fairford. We had to take
measurements forty foot underneath it taking off...quite noisy.
I think it's great and always have done.'*

Andy [surname withheld] Telephone engineer

'It's a British icon, innit? I'm not a plane-spotter, I'm just jumping on the bandwagon to shoot some film of it at an amateur level....'

Tuomas Rasanen (28) Student, from Finland

'It's the most greatest and beautiful aircraft I have ever seen. I came here for four days, not just to see Concorde but also to buy Concorde books.'

Colin Skilton (67) Retired work study officer

'It's ugly... the ugly daughter of the Vulcan Bomber.'

Thomas White (18) Morrison's supermarket worker

'It goes supersonic, is good-looking, and has luxurious accommodation.'

Geoff Shew (58) Painter and decorator

'It's sad to see the loss of the last thing that made Britain great.'

Jamie Kitson (18) Nurse

'[Concorde is] something that never fails to amaze, however many times you see it....
It can entertain the most bored of people.'

Wayne [surname withheld] Van driver

'I shouldn't be here, as I should be at work. It's absolutely gutting what they're doing with it.'

Robert Moore (44) Manchester cab driver

'I come here three times a year for three or four days.... It's a nice break from my girlfriend.'

Mr Finch (51) Plastics factory worker from Norwich

'I came down for the day.'

[Name withheld]

'I'm just trying this for the day to see if I like it....'

Simon Axtem (38) Systems analyst

'I just wanted to say goodbye.'

Stuart Bourne (63) Photographic printer

'It's a wonderful aerodynamic lady....'

Paul Veir [age withheld] Canadian Navy (retired)

'I came to England to see my mother and thought I would come and see Concorde.... It's a shame.'

Peter Zabek (51) Photographer

'To see it take off in particular is awesome.'

Gary Winspear (43) Carpenter, from Birmingham

'Unique. It's my last chance to see it operational, so I came down.'

Nick Sharpley (29) IT professional, from Australia

'From my point of view we don't have anything like it in Australia. It's a legend....
To see the legend...what more could you hope for?'

Louisa Evans (26) British Airways worker at Heathrow Airport

'What a magnificent bird.'

Ray Mills (68) Semi-retired wedding photographer

*'It's a pity really because it's such a prestige thing....
Even though it's fifty per cent French, it's a British icon.'*

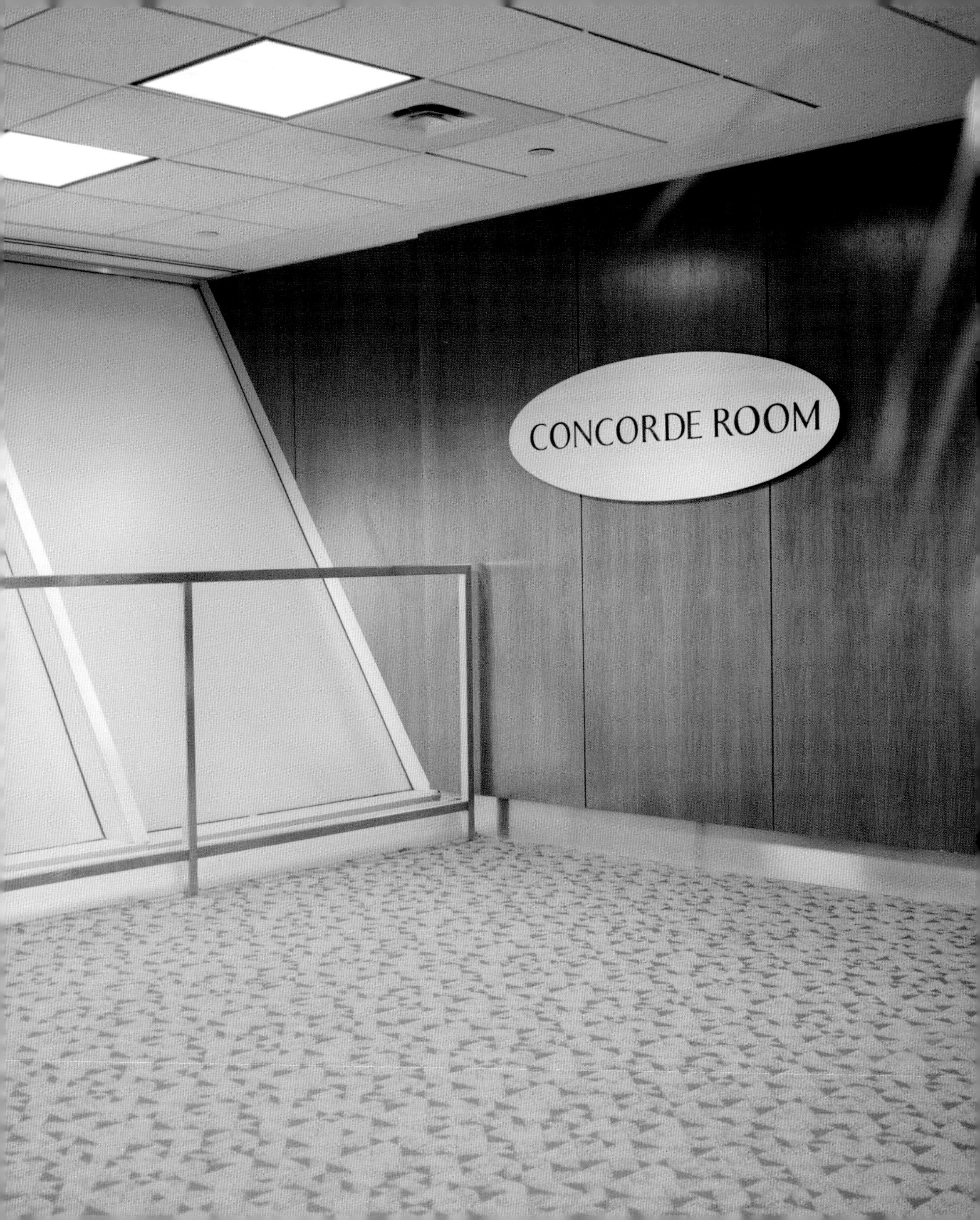
CONCORDE ROOM

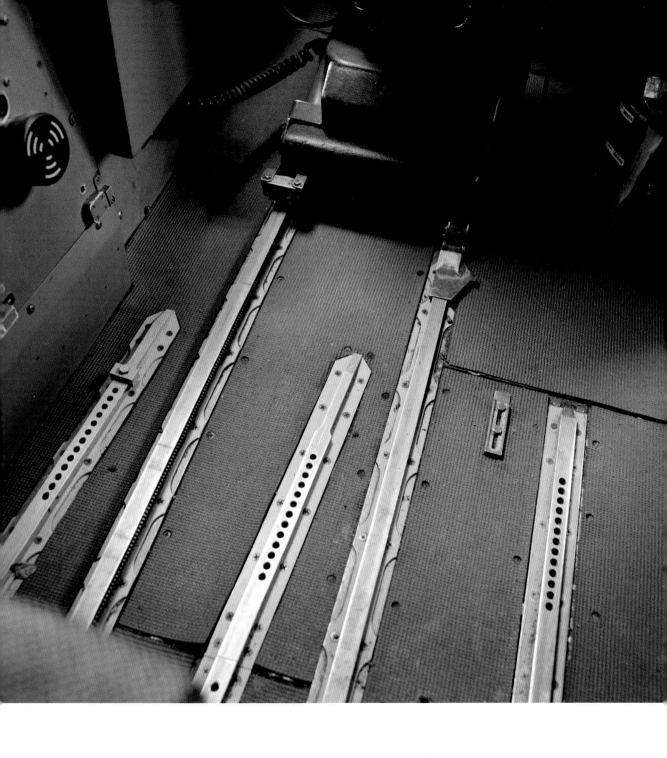

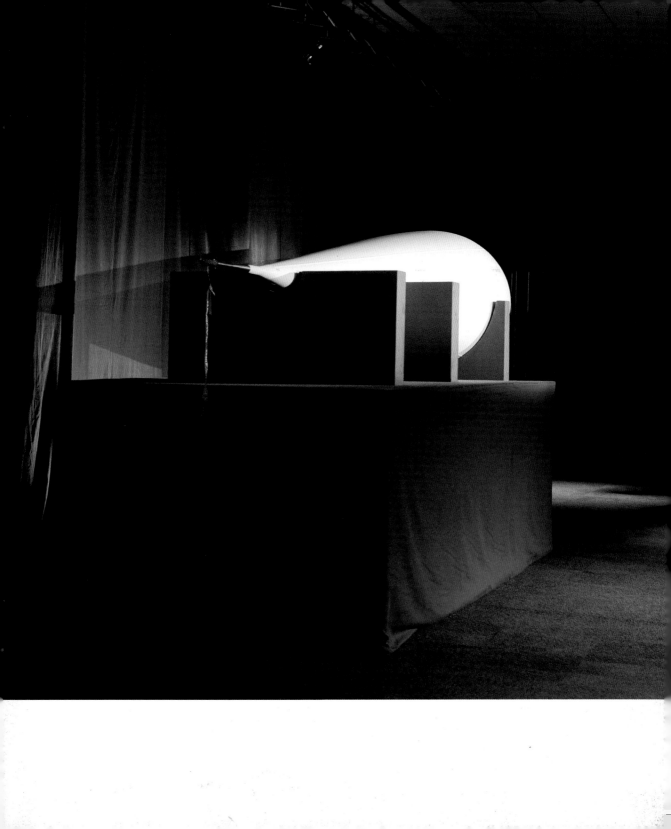